# INSPIRATIONAL

# Poems

# ABOUT

# LIFE and SUCCESS

**Thought-provoking and empowering
words to uplift and inspire you**

**Verusha Singh**

Published by
Ink 'n Ivory
P O Box 6321, Rouse Hill, NSW. 2155. Australia

www.inkNivory.com
Printed in Australia

First Printing:  2014
ISBN: 978-1-922113-11-5 (Paperback)
ISBN: 978-1-922113-13-9 (Mobi)
ISBN: 978-1-922113-12-2 (ePub)

Disclaimer

This publication is shared with the understanding that the publisher and author are not engaged in rendering financial, psychological or any other professional service and is offered for information purposes only. If financial or any other professional advice or assistance is required, the services of a competent professional person should be sought. The reader is solely responsible for his/her own actions arising from the use of this document.

# Introduction

Many poems, and poets for that matter, earn fame because of their ability to inspire others. They had the keen ability to use the written word to reach hearts and souls, motivating people to action. Inspiration comes in many forms. However, the root of all inspiration is the idea that our lives are meaningful. Inspiration is knowing that what I do matters deeply to the universe. When you have the feeling that your actions are meaningful, you will become filled with strength and vigor to fulfill your life's purpose.

Inspirational poems enable us to see the world in new ways, whether offering hope for a better future, speaking of faith in a loving god or depicting the beauty of nature and the innate goodness of mankind. The profound poems in this book will touch your heart and inspire you to open to your deeper potential in life.

# The Little Chap Who Follows Me

A careful man I want to be;
A little fellow follows me.
I do not dare to go astray
For fear he'll go the self same way.
I cannot once escape his eyes,
Whate'er he sees me do, he tries.
Like me he says he's going to be;
The little chap who follows me.
He thinks that I'm so very fine,
Believes in every word of mine.
The base in me he must not see;
The little chap who follows me.
I must remember as I go
Through summer's sun and winter's snow,
I'm building for the years to be;
The little chap who follows me.

~ Unknown

# The Cookie Thief

A woman was waiting at an airport one night,
With several long hours before her flight.
She hunted for a book in the airport shops.
Bought a bag of cookies and found a place to drop.

She was engrossed in her book but happened to see,
That the man sitting beside her, as bold as could be.
Grabbed a cookie or two from the bag in between,
Which she tried to ignore to avoid a scene.

So she munched the cookies and watched the clock,
As the gutsy cookie thief diminished her stock.
She was getting more irritated as the minutes ticked by,
Thinking, "If I wasn't so nice, I would blacken his eye."

With each cookie she took, he took one too,
When only one was left, she wondered what he would do.
With a smile on his face, and a nervous laugh,
He took the last cookie and broke it in half.

He offered her half, as he ate the other,
She snatched it from him and thought... oooh, brother.
This guy has some nerve and he's also rude,
Why he didn't even show any gratitude!

She had never known when she had been so galled,
And sighed with relief when her flight was called.
She gathered her belongings and headed to the gate,
Refusing to look back at the thieving ingrate.

She boarded the plane, and sank in her seat,
Then she sought her book, which was almost complete.
As she reached in her baggage, she gasped with surprise,
There was her bag of cookies, in front of her eyes.

If mine are here, she moaned in despair,
The others were his, and he tried to share.
Too late to apologize, she realized with grief,
That she was the rude one, the ingrate, the thief.

~ Valerie Cox

If there is light in the soul,
There will be beauty in the person.
If there is beauty in the person,
There will be harmony in the house.
If there is harmony in the house,
There will be order in the nation.
If there is order in the nation,
There will be peace in the world.

~ Chinese Proverb

# The Comfort Zone

I used to have a comfort zone where I knew I wouldn't fail.
The same four walls and busywork were really more like jail.
I longed so much to do the things I'd never done before,
But stayed inside my comfort zone and paced the same old floor.

I said it didn't matter that I wasn't doing much.
I said I didn't care for things like commission cheques and such.
I claimed to be so busy with things inside my zone,
But deep inside I longed for something special of my own.

I couldn't let my life go by just watching others win.
I held my breath; I stepped outside and let the change begin.
I took a step and with new strength I'd never felt before,
I kissed my comfort zone goodbye and closed and locked the door.

If you're in a comfort zone, afraid to venture out,
Remember that all winners were at one time filled with doubt.
A step or two and words of praise can make your dreams come true.
Reach for your future with a smile; success is there for you!

~ Anonymous

# Be The Best of Whatever You Are

If you can't be a pine on the top of the hill,
Be a scrub in the valley, but be…
The best little scrub by the side of the rill;
Be a bush if you can't be a tree.

If you can't be a bush be a bit of the grass,
And some highway happier make;
If you can't be a muskie then just be a bass
But the liveliest bass in the lake!

We can't all be captains, we've got to be crew,
There's something for all of us here,
There's big work to do, and there's lesser to do,
And the task you must do is the near.

If you can't be a highway then just be a trail,
If you can't be the sun be a star;
It isn't by size that you win or you fail
Be the best of whatever you are!

~ Douglas Malloch

## *Lessons from an Oyster*

There once was an oyster
Whose story I tell,
Who found that some sand
Had got into his shell.

It was only a grain,
but it gave him great pain.
For oysters have feelings
Although they're so plain.

Now, did he berate
the harsh workings of fate
That had brought him
To such a deplorable state?

Did he curse at the government,
Cry for election,
And claim that the sea should
Have given him protection?

'No,' he said to himself
As he lay on a shell,
Since I cannot remove it,
I shall try to improve it.

Now the years have rolled around,
As the years always do,
And he came to his ultimate
Destiny stew.

And the small grain of sand
That had bothered him so
Was a beautiful pearl
All richly aglow.

Now the tale has a moral,
for isn't it grand
What an oyster can do
With a morsel of sand?

What couldn't we do
If we'd only begin
With some of the things
That get under our skin.

~ Unknown

Not what we give, but what we share,
For the gift without the giver is bare.

~ James Russell Lowell

## Stick To Your Job

Diamonds are only chunks of coal
That stuck to their jobs, you see;
If they'd petered out, as most of us do,
Where would the diamonds be?
It isn't the fact of making a start,
It's the sticking that counts, I'll say;
It's the fellow that knows not the meaning of fail,
But hammers and hammers away.
Whenever you think that you've come to the end,
And you're beaten as bad as can be,
Remember that diamonds are chunks of coal
That stuck to their jobs you see.

~ Minnie Richard Smith

Even after all this time,
The Sun never says to the earth:
"You owe me!"
Look at what happens with,
A love like that!
It lights the whole sky!

~ Hafiz

No Vision and you perish;
No Ideal, and you're last;
Your heart must ever Cherish,
Some Faith at any cost.
Some hope, some Dream to cling to,
Some Rainbow in the sky,
Some Melody to sing to,
Some Service that is high.

~ Harriet Du Autermont

# Comparisons

If you've never trod the valley,
You can never see the heights,
If you've never walked in darkness,
You'll never see the light,

If you do not climb the hill ahead,
You can't look round the bend,
If you're never really lonely,
You'll never need a friend,

If you've never failed, and failed again,
You'll never try your best,
If you've never suffered sleeplessness,
You'll never know true rest,

If you've never stumbled through the clouds,
You'll never see the blue,
If you've never suffered grief or pain,
Real joy won't come to you,

For the one calls forth the other,
As onward we must go,
Don't ask me how I found this out,
Let me just say "I know".

~ Unknown

# The Cold Within

Six humans trapped by happenstance
in bleak and bitter cold.
Each one possessed a stick of wood
or so the story's told.

Their dying fire in need of logs
but a white man held his back.
For of the faces round the fire
he noticed one was black.

The next man looking cross the way
saw one not of his church.
And couldn't bring himself to give
the fire his stick of birch.

The third one sat in tattered clothes
he gave his coat a hitch.
Why should his log be put to use
to warm the idle rich?

The rich man just sat back and thought
of the wealth he had in store.
And how to keep what he had earned
from the lazy, shiftless poor.

The black man's face bespoke revenge
as the fire passed from his sight.
For all he saw in his stack of wood
was a chance to spite the white.

The last man of this forlorn group
did naught except for gain.
Giving only to those who gave
was how he played the game.

Their logs held tight in death's still hand
was proof of human sin.
They did not die from the cold outside
they died from the cold within.

~ Jay Patrick Kinney

If you love a flower, don't pick it up.
Because if you pick it up it dies
and it ceases to be what you love.
So if you love a flower, let it be.
Love is not about possession.
Love it about appreciation.

~ Osho

# Thinking

If you think you are beaten, you are
If you think you dare not, you don't,
If you like to win, but you think you can't
It is almost certain you won't.

If you think you'll lose, you've lost
For out of the world we find,
Success begins with a fellow's will
It's all in the state of mind.

If you think you are outclassed, you are
You've got to think high to rise,
You've got to be sure of yourself before
You can ever win a prize.

Life's battles don't always go
To the stronger or faster man,
But soon or late the man who wins
Is the man WHO THINKS HE CAN!

~ Walter D. Wintle

# *Victory*

You are the Man who used to boast
that you'd achieve the uttermost,
some day.

You merely wished to show,
to demonstrate how much you know
and prove the distance you can go..

Another year we've just passed through.
What new ideas came to you?
How many big things did you do?

Time left twelve fresh months in your care
how many of them did you share
with opportunity and dare
again where you so often missed?

We do not find you on the list of makers good.
explain the fact!
Ah No, 'Twas not the chance you lacked!
As usual - you failed to act!

~ Herbert Kauffman

# The Laggard's Excuse

He worked by day
And toiled by night,
He gave up play
And some delight.
Dry books he read
New things to learn
And forged ahead,
Success to earn.
He plodded on
With faith and pluck,
And when he won
Men called it luck.

~ Unknown

# M. Guffey's Primer

Work while you work,
Play while you play;
One thing each time,
That is the way.
All that you do,
Do with your might;
Things done by halves
Are not done right!

~ Unknown

## Sermons We See

I'd rather see a sermon
than hear one any day;
I'd rather one should walk with me
than merely tell the way.

The eye's a better pupil
and more willing than the ear,
Fine counsel is confusing,
but example's always clear;

And the best of all the preachers
are the men who live their creeds,
For to see good put in action
is what everybody needs.

I soon can learn to do it
if you'll let me see it done;
I can watch your hands in action,
but your tongue too fast may run.

And the lecture you deliver
may be very wise and true,
But I'd rather get my lessons
by observing what you do;

For I might misunderstand you
and the high advice you give,
But there's no misunderstanding
how you act and how you live.

When I see a deed of kindness,
I am eager to be kind.
When a weaker brother stumbles
and a strong man stays behind

Just to see if he can help him,
then the wish grows strong in me
To become as big and thoughtful
as I know that friend to be.

And all travelers can witness
that the best of guides today
Is not the one who tells them,
but the one who shows the way.

One good man teaches many,
men believe what they behold;
One deed of kindness noticed
is worth forty that are told.

Who stands with men of honor
learns to hold his honor dear,
For right living speaks a language
which to every one is clear.

Though an able speaker charms me
with his eloquence, I say,
I'd rather see a sermon
than to hear one, any day.

~ Edgar A. Guest

# Thoughts Are Things

I hold it true that thoughts are things,
They're endowed with bodies and breath and wings:
And that we send them forth to fill
The world with good results, or ill.
That which we call our secret thought
Speeds forth to Earth's remotest spot,
Leaving its blessings or woes
Like tracks behind as it goes.
We build our future, thought by thought,
For good or ill, yet know it not.
Yet so the Universe was wrought.
Thought is another name for fate;
Choose then thy destiny and wait,
For love brings love and hate brings hate.

~ Henry Van Dyke

# If

If you can keep your head when all about you
Are losing theirs and blaming it on you;
If you can trust yourself when all men doubt you,
But make allowance for their doubting too;
If you can wait and not be tired of waiting,
Or, being lied about, don't deal in lies,
Or, being hated, don't give way to hating,
And yet don't look too good, not talk too wise;

If you can dream – and not make dreams your master
If you can think – and not make thoughts your aim;
If you can meet with triumph and disaster
And treat those two impostors just the same;
If you can bear to hear the truth you've spoken
Twisted by knaves to make a trap for fools,
Or watch the things you gave your life to broken,
And stoop and build 'em up with worn-out tools;

If you can make one heap of all your winnings
And risk it on one turn of pitch-and-toss,
And lose, and start again at your beginnings
And never breathe a word about your loss;
If you can force your heart and nerve and sinew
To serve your turn long after they are gone,
And so hold on when there is nothing in you
Except the Will, which says to them: "Hold on";

If you can talk with crowds and keep your virtue,
Or walk with kings – nor lose the common touch;
If neither foes nor loving friends can hurt you;
If all men count with you, but none too much;
If you can fill the unforgiving minute
With sixty seconds' worth of distance run-Yours
is the Earth and everything that's in it,
And – which is more – you'll be a Man, my son!

~ Rudyard Kipling

Faith, mighty faith
The promise sees
And looks to God alone,
Laughs at impossibilities
And cries, 'It shall be done.'

~ Unknown

# The Invitation

It doesn't interest me what you do for a living; I want to know what you ache for and if you dare to dream of meeting your hearts longing.

It doesn't interest me how old you are, I want to know if you will risk looking like a fool for love, for your dream, for the adventure of being alive.

It doesn't interest me what planets are squaring your moon, I want to know if you have touched the center of your sorrow, if you have been opened by life's betrayals or have become shriveled and closed from fear of further pain.

I want to know if you can sit with pain, mine or your own; without moving to hide it or fade it, or fix it. I want to know if you can be with joy mine or your own; and if you can dance with wildness and let the ecstasy fill you to the tips of your fingers and toes without cautioning us to be careful, be realistic, or to remember the limitations of being human.

It doesn't interest me if the story you are telling me is true, I want to know if you can disappoint another to be true to yourself, if you can bear the accusation of betrayal and not betray your own soul.

I want to know if you can be faithful and therefore trustworthy, I want to know if you can

see the beauty even when it is not pretty every day
and if you can source your life on the edge of the
lake and shout to the silver of the full moon.

It doesn't interest me to know where you live or
how much money you have, I want to know if you
can get up after a night of grief and despair, weary
and bruised to the bone and do what needs to done
for the children.

It doesn't interest me to know who you know or how
you came to be here, I want to know if you will stand
on the center of fire with me and not shrink back.

It doesn't interest me where or what or with whom
you have studied, I want to know what sustains you
from the inside when all else falls away.

I want to know if you can be alone with yourself
and if you truly like the company you keep in the
empty moments

~ Oriah Mountain Dreamer

# My Wage

I bargained with Life for a penny,
And Life would pay no more,
However I begged at evening
When I counted my scanty store;

For Life is a just employer,
He gives you what you ask,
But once you have set the wages,
Why, you must bear the task.

I worked for a menial's hire,
Only to learn, dismayed,
That any wage I had asked of Life,
Life would have gladly paid.

~ Jessie B Rittenhouse

# The Meaning Of Service

The Sea of Galilee
and the Dead Sea are
made of the same water.
It flows down,
clear and cool,
from the heights of Hermon
and the roots of
the cedars of Lebanon.
The Sea of Galilee
makes beauty of it,
for the Sea of Galilee
has an outlet.
It gets to give.
It gathers in its riches that
it may pour them out again
to fertilise the Jordan plain.
But the Dead Sea with the
same water makes horror.
For the Dead Sea
has no outlet.
It gets to keep.

~ Henry Emerson Fosdick

# Be Thankful

Be thankful that you don't already have everything you desire.
If you did, what would there be to look forward to?

Be thankful when you don't know something,
for it gives you the opportunity to learn.

Be thankful for the difficult times.
During those times you grow.

Be thankful for your limitations,
because they give you opportunities for improvement.

Be thankful for each new challenge,
because it will build your strength and character.

Be thankful for your mistakes.
They will teach you valuable lessons.

Be thankful when you're tired and weary,
because it means you've made a difference.

It's easy to be thankful for the good things.
A life of rich fulfillment comes to those who
are also thankful for the setbacks.

Gratitude can turn a negative into a positive.
Find a way to be thankful for your troubles,
and they can become your blessings.

~ Unknown

# Count Your Blessings

If you woke up this morning with more health than illness you are more blessed than the million who will not survive this week.

If you have never experienced the danger of battle, the loneliness of imprisonment, the agony of torture, or the pangs of starvation you are ahead of 500 million people in the world.

If you can attend a church meeting without fear of harassment, arrest, torture, or death you are more blessed than three billion people in the world.

If you have food in the refrigerator, clothes on your back, a roof overhead and a place to sleep you are richer than 75% of this world.

If you have money in the bank, in your wallet, and spare change in a dish someplace you are among the top 8% of the world's wealthy.

If your parents are still alive and still married you are very rare, even in the United States and Canada.

If you can read this message, you just received a double blessing in that someone was thinking of you, and furthermore, you are more blessed than over two billion people in the world that cannot read at all.

~ Unknown

# A Smile

A smile costs nothing, but gives much-
It takes but a moment, but the memory of it
usually lasts forever.
None are so rich that can get along without it-
And none are so poor but that can be made rich
by it.

It enriches those who receive, without making
poor those who give-
It creates sunshine in the home,
Fosters good will in business,
And is the best antidote for trouble-
And yet it cannot be begged, borrowed, or stolen,
for it is of no value
Unless it is given away.

Some people are too busy to give you a smile-
Give them one of yours-
For the good Lord knows that no one needs a
smile so badly
As he or she who has no more smiles left to give.

~ Unknown

## Just One

One song can spark a moment,
One flower can wake the dream
One tree can start a forest,
One bird can herald spring.

One smile begins a friendship,
One handclasp lifts a soul.
One star can guide a ship at sea,
One word can frame the goal

One vote can change a nation,
One sunbeam lights a room
One candle wipes out darkness,
One laugh will conquer gloom.

One step must start each journey.
One word must start each prayer.
One hope will raise our spirits,
One touch can show you care.

One voice can speak with wisdom,
One heart can know what's true,
One life can make a difference,
You see, it's up to you!

~ Unknown

# If I Had my Child To Raise Over Again

If I had my child to raise all over again,
I'd build self-esteem first, and the house later.
I'd finger paint more, and point the finger less.
I would do less correcting and more connecting.

I'd take my eyes off my watch, and watch with my eyes.
I would care to know less and know to care more.
I'd take more hikes and fly more kites.
I'd stop playing serious, and seriously play.

I would run through more fields and gaze at more stars,
I'd do more hugging and less tugging.
I'd see the oak tree in the acorn more often,
I would be firm less often, and affirm much more.

I'd model less about the love of power,
And more about the power of love.

~ Diane Loomans

# The Man In The Glass

When you get what you want in your struggle for self
And the world makes you king for a day,
Just go to the mirror and look at yourself
And see what that man has to say.

For it isn't your father or mother or wife
Whose judgment upon you must pass.
The fellow whose verdict counts most in you life
Is the one staring back from the glass.

You may be like Jack Horner and chisel a plum
And think you're a wonderful guy.
But the man in the glass says you're only a bum
If you can't look him straight in the eye.

He's the fellow to please-never mind all the rest,
For he's with you clear to the end.
And you've passed your most dangerous, difficult test
If the man in the glass is your friend.

You may fool the whole world down the pathway of years
And get pats on the back as you pass.
But your final reward will be heartache and tears
If you've cheated the man in the glass.

~ Dale Wimbrow

# The Right Kind Of People

Gone is the city, gone the day,
Yet still the story and the meaning stay:
Once where a prophet in the palm shade basked
A traveler chanced at noon to rest his miles.

"What sort of people may they be," he asked,
"In this proud city on the plains o'erspread?"
"Well, friend, what sort of people whence you came?"
"What sort?" the packman scowled; "why, knaves and
fools."
"You'll find the people here the same," the wise man said.

Another stranger in the dusk drew near,
And pausing, cried "What sort of people here
In your bright city where yon towers arise?"
"Well, friend, what sort of people whence you came?"
"What sort?" the pilgrim smiled,
"Good, true and wise."
"You'll find the people here the same," The wise man said.

~ Edwin Markham

## *Don't Quit*

When things go wrong as they sometimes will,
When the road you're trudging seems all uphill.
When the funds are low and the debts are high,
And you want to smile, but you have to sigh.
When care is pressing you down a bit,
Rest if you must, but don't you quit.

Life is queer with its twists and turns,
As every one of us sometimes learns.
And many a fellow turns about,
When he might have won had he stuck it out.
Don't give up though the pace seems slow,
You may succeed with another blow.

Often the goal is nearer than
It seems to a faint and faltering man.
Often the struggler has given up,
When he might have captured the victor's cup.
And he learned too late when the night came down,
How close he was to the golden crown.

Success is failure turned inside out,
The silver tint of the clouds of doubt.
And you never can tell how close you are,
It may be near when it seems afar.
So stick to the fight when you're hardest hit,
It's when things seem worst that you mustn't quit.

~ Unknown

# The Little Red Hen

Said the big white rooster, 'Gosh all Hemlock, things
are tough,
Seems that worms are getting scarce and I cannot find
enough.
What's become of all those fat ones is a mystery to me;
There were thousands through the rainy spell, but now
where can they be?'

The little red hen, who heard him, didn't grumble or
complain,
She had been through lots of dry spells, she had lived
through floods of rain;
So she flew up on the grindstone and she gave her
claws a whet,
And she said, I've never seen a time there were no
worms to get.

She picked a new and undug spot; the earth was hard
and firm.
The big white rooster jeered, New ground! That's no
place for a worm.
The little red hen spread her feet, she dug fast and free,
'I must go to the worms," she said, 'the worms won't
come to me.

The rooster vainly spent his day, through habit by the ways,
Where fat worms have passed in squads, back in the rainy days.
When nightfall found him supperless, he growled in accents rough,
'I'm as hungry as a fowl can be. Conditions sure are tough.'

He turned to the little red hen and said, 'It's worse with you,
For you're not only hungry, but you must be tired too.
I rested while I watched for worms, so I feel fairly perk;
But how are you? Without worms, too? And after all that work?

The little red hen hopped to her perch and dropped her eyes to sleep,
And murmured, in a drowsy tone, 'Young man, hear this and weep,
I'm full of worms and happy, for I've dined both long and well,
The worms were there, as always, but I had to dig like hell!'

Oh, here and there white roosters are still holding sales positions,
They cannot do much business now, because of poor conditions.
But as soon as things get right again, they'll sell a hundred firms,
Meanwhile, the little red hens are out, a-gobbling up the worms.

~ Unknown

# Dancing With God

When I meditated on the word Guidance,
I kept seeing 'dance' at the end of the word.

I remember reading that doing God's will is a lot like
dancing.
When two people try to lead, nothing feels right.
The movement doesn't flow with the music,
and everything is quite uncomfortable and jerky.

When one person realizes that, and lets the other lead,
both bodies begin to flow with the music.
One gives gentle cues, perhaps with a nudge to the back
or by pressing Lightly in one direction or another.

It's as if two become one body, moving beautifully.
The dance takes surrender, willingness,
and attentiveness from one person
and gentle guidance and skill from the other.

My eyes drew back to the word Guidance.
When I saw 'G': I thought of God, followed by 'u' and 'i'.
'God, 'u' and 'i' dance.'
God, you, and I dance.

As I lowered my head, I became willing to trust
that I would get guidance about my life.
Once again, I became willing to let God lead.
My prayer for you today is that God's blessings
and mercies are upon you on this day and everyday.

May you abide in God, as God abides in you.
Dance together with God, trusting God to lead
and to guide you through each season of your life.
If God has done anything for you in your life,
please share this message with someone else.

There is no cost but a lot of rewards;
so let's continue to pray for one another.
And I Hope You Dance !

~ Unknown

Only as high as I reach can I grow,
only as far as I seek can I go,
only as deep as I look can I see,
only as much as I dream can I be.

~ Karen Ravn

# The Indispensable Man

Sometimes, when you're feeling important,
Sometimes, when your ego's in bloom,
Sometimes, when you take it for granted
You're the best qualified in the room.

Sometimes, when you feel that your going
Would leave an unfilled hole,
Just follow this simple instruction,
and see how it humbles your soul:

Take a bucket and fill it with water,
Put your hand in it up to the wrist,
Pull it out and the hole that's remaining
Is a measure of how you'll be missed.

You may splash all you please when you enter,
You can stir up the water galore,
But stop, and you'll find in a minute
That it looks quite the same as before.

The moral of this quaint example
Is to do just the best that you can;
Be proud of yourself, but remember,
There is no indispensable man.(or woman)

~ Saxon White Kessinger

# The Will To Win

If you want a thing bad enough
To go out and fight for it,
Work day and night for it,
Give up your time and your peace and your sleep for it

If only desire of it
Makes you quite mad enough
Never to tire of it,
Makes you hold all other things tawdry
and cheap for it

If life seems all empty and useless without it
And all that you scheme and you dream is about it,
If gladly you'll sweat for it,
Fret for it, Plan for it,

Lose all your terror of God or man for it,
If you'll simply go after that thing that you want.
With all your capacity,
Strength and sagacity,

Faith, hope and confidence, stern pertinacity,
If neither cold poverty, famished and gaunt,
Nor sickness nor pain
Of body or brain

Can turn you away from the thing that you want,
If dogged and grim you besiege and beset it,
You'll get it!

~ Berton Braley

## Success

He has achieved success who has lived well,
laughed often, and loved much;

who has enjoyed the trust of pure women,
the respect of intelligent men
and the love of little children;

who has filled his niche and accomplished his task;

who has left the world better than he found it
whether by an improved poppy,
a perfect poem or a rescued soul;

who has never lacked appreciation of Earth's beauty
or failed to express it;

who has always looked for the best in others
and given them the best he had;

whose life was an inspiration;
whose memory a benediction.

~ Bessie Anderson Stanley

# Courage

Courage is not only gifted to the few brave ones,
It is something that lies within you,
Where you can draw upon its strength and power,
In times of crisis, fears and decisions.

Courage is not something mysterious or
unattainable,
It is something that you can exercise in your daily
life choices,
You can let it bring to you untraveled paths,
And make you more conscious and aware of your
life.

Courage does not have to roar to be heard,
It does not mean being totally fearless and being
invincible,
It could mean taking actions, taking risks, taking a
stand,
Standing up for yourself, standing by your choices,
And sticking to your dreams when others jeered.

Courage could be the will to live in spite of the
struggles,
In spite of your fears and phobias, in spite of
what others said,
In spite of criticisms and disapproval, in spite of
mistakes and failures,
In spite of everything that stands between you
and your dreams.

Courage could mean trying over and over again
when you failed,
Admitting that you are sorry when you are in the
wrong,
Saying I love you when your love is angry,
Having a baby when the idea of being a parent
scared you,
Listening to your heart when others called you a
fool,
Following your dreams even when others
discouraged you,
And staying true to yourself when others want you
in another way.

Hold steadfast to your dreams, your heart and
yourself,
And courage will not abandon you,
But follows you whenever you choose to go.

~ Fion Lim

# The Game of Life

Life is a game
And like any game
There are rules.
You can play to win
Or you can play to lose…
And you always get to choose.
But whether you win, or you lose
Will depend on how you apply the rules.
The rules are mysterious, even baffling at times.
Often you will say that you are doing all you can do,
But your results will tell 'that is not true'
Because you have breached the rules
For which you must pay the price
And repeat the lesson
Till you have learned it right.
Only then will you win
The game of life!

~ Verusha Singh

## Risky Business

It's a risk to have a husband,
it's a risk to have a son;
It's a risk to pour your confidences out to anyone;
It's a risk to pick a daisy,
for there's sure to be a cop;
It's a risk to go on living,
but a greater risk to stop.

~ Ruth Mason Rice

If you were busy being kind,
Before you knew it, you would find
You'd soon forget to think 'twas true
That someone was unkind to you.
If you were busy being glad,
And cheering people who are sad,
Although your heart might ache a bit,
You'd soon forget to notice it.

~ R. Foreman

# Life

They told me that Life could be just what I made it
Life could be fashioned and worn like a gown;
I, the designer, mine the decision
Whether to wear it with bonnet or crown.

And so I selected the prettiest pattern
Life should be made of the rosiest hue
Something unique, and a bit out of fashion,
One that perhaps would be chosen by few.

But other folks came and they leaned o'er my
shoulder;
Someone questioned the ultimate cost;
Somebody tangled the thread I was using;
One day I found that my scissors were lost.

And somebody claimed the material faded;
Somebody said I'd be tired ere 'twas worn;
Somebody's fingers, too pointed and spiteful,
Snatched at the cloth, and I saw it was torn.

Oh! somebody tried to do all the sewing,
Wanting always to advise or condone.
Here is my life, the product of many;
Where is that gown I could fashion - alone?

~ Nan Terrell Reed

# Count That Day Lost

If you sit down at set of sun,
And count the acts that you have done,
And, counting, find
One self-denying deed, one word,

That eased the heart of him who heard,
One glance most kind
That fell like sunshine where it went,
Then you may count that day well spent.

But if, through all the livelong day,
You've cheered no heart, by yea or nay.
If, through it all
You've nothing done that you can trace

That brought the sunshine to one face,
No act most small
That helped some soul and nothing cost,
Then count that day as worse than lost.

~ George Eliot

# Influence

Drop a pebble in the water,
And its ripples reach out far;
And the sunbeams dancing on them
May reflect them to a star.

Give a smile to someone passing,
Thereby making his morning glad;
It may greet you in the evening
When your own heart may be sad.

Do a deed of simple kindness;
Though its end you may not see,
It may reach, like widening ripples,
Down a long eternity.

~ Joseph Norris

# The Road Less Travelled

Two roads diverged in a yellow wood,
And sorry I could not travel both
And be one traveler, long I stood
And looked down one as far as I could
To where it bent in the undergrowth;
Then took the other, as just as fair,
And having perhaps the better claim,
Because it was grassy and wanted wear;
Though as for that the passing there
Had worn them really about the same,
And both that morning equally lay
In leaves no step had trodden black.
Oh, I kept the first for another day!
Yet knowing how way leads on to way,
I doubted if I should ever come back.
I shall be telling this with a sigh
Somewhere ages and ages hence:
Two roads diverged in a wood, and II
took the one less traveled by,
And that has made all the difference.

~ Robert Frost

# The Test of a Man

The test of a man is the fight he makes,
The grit that he daily shows;
The way he stands on his feet and takes
Fate's numerous bumps and blows.

A coward can smile when there's naught to fear,
When nothing his progress bars;
But it takes a man to stand up and cheer
While some other fellow stars.

It isn't the victory, after all,
But the fight that a brother makes;
The man who, driven against the wall,
Still stands up erect and takes

The blows of fate with his head held high;
Bleeding, and bruised, and pale,
Is the man who'll win in the by and by,
For he isn't afraid to fail.

It's the bumps you get, and the jolts you get,
And the shocks that your courage stands,
The hours of sorrow and vain regret,
The prize that escapes your hands,

That test your mettle and prove your worth;
It isn't the blows you deal,
But the blows you take on the good old earth,
That show if your stuff is real.

~ Unknown

# It Couldn't be Done

Somebody said that it couldn't be done,
But, he with a chuckle replied
That "maybe it couldn't" but he would be one
Who wouldn't say so till he'd tried.

So he buckled right in with the trace of a grin
On his face. If he worried he hid it.
He started to sing as he tackled the thing
That couldn't be done, as he did it.

Somebody scoffed: "Oh, you'll never do that;
At least no one we know has done it";
But he took off his coat and he took off his hat,
And the first thing we knew he'd begun it.

With a lift of his chin and a bit of a grin,
Without any doubting or quiddit,
He started to sing as he tackled the thing
That couldn't be done, and he did it.

There are thousands to tell you it cannot be done,
There are thousands to prophesy failure;
There are thousands to point out to you, one by one,
The dangers that wait to assail you.

But just buckle right in with a bit of a grin,
Just take off your coat and go to it;
Just start to sing as you tackle the thing
That cannot be done, and you'll do it.

~ Edgar Guest

# *Forgive Me When I Whine*

Today, upon a bus,
I saw a lovely girl with golden hair.
I envied her. She seemed so happy;
I wished I were as fair.

When suddenly she rose to leave,
I saw her hobble down the aisle;
She had one leg and wore a crutch;
But as she passed...a smile!

Oh, God forgive me when I whine,
I have two legs. The world is mine!

I stopped to buy some candy.
The lad who sold it had such charm.
I talked with him. He seemed so glad.
If I were late it would do no harm.
And as I left he said to me,
'I thank you; You have been so kind.
It's nice to talk with folks like you.
You see,' he said, "I'm blind.'

Oh, God forgive me when I whine,
I have two eyes. The world is mine!

Later while walking down the street,
I saw a child with eyes of blue.
He stood and watched the others play,
he did not know what to do.
I stopped a moment and said,

"Why don't you join the others, dear?"
He looked ahead without a word and then I knew,
he couldn't hear.

Oh, God forgive me when I whine,
I have two ears, the world is mine.
With feet to take me where I go,
with eyes to see the sun-set glow,
with ears to hear what I would know.
Oh, God forgive me when I whine,
I am blessed indeed, the world is mine!

~ Red Foley

## We Must

We must be silent before we can listen.
We must listen before we can learn.
We must learn before we can prepare.
We must prepare before we can serve.
We must serve before we can lead.

~ William Arthur Ward

## *Persistence*

I must persist if I am to rise.
Life's challenge I see before my eyes,
I set my sights on a worthy task,
That makes me reach beyond my grasp.

Those who persist will often fall,
For a child to walk he first must crawl,
Try he will, till he finds his feet,
He has not yet learnt the word defeat.

Such childish ignorance makes man great,
But learnt too soon, will seal his fate.
When your heart has will, yourself provoke,
From a seed you'll grow to a mighty oak.

~ C.N Andre Day

# Do Less

Do less thinking,
And pay more attention to your heart
Do less acquiring,
And pay more attention to what you already have
Do less complaining,
And pay more attention to giving
Do less controlling,
And pay more attention to letting go
Do less criticizing,
And pay more attention to complimenting
Do less arguing,
And pay more attention to forgiveness
Do less running around,
And pay more attention to stillness
Do less talking,
And pay more attention to silence.

~ Unknown

## *Success*

Success is speaking words of praise,
In cheering other people's ways.
In doing just the best you can,
With every task and every plan.

It's silence when your speech would hurt,
Politeness when your neighbor's curt.
It's deafness when the scandal flows,
And sympathy with others' woes.

It's loyalty when duty calls,
It's courage when disaster falls.
It's patience when the hours are long,
It's found in laughter and in song.

It's in the silent time of prayer,
In happiness and in despair.
In all of life and nothing less,
We find the thing we call success.

~ Unknown

## Prayer

I asked for strength and
God gave me difficulties to make me strong
I asked for wisdom and
God gave me problems to solve

I asked for prosperity and
God gave me brawn and brains to work
I asked for courage and
God gave me dangers to overcome

I asked for patience and
God placed me in situations where I was
forced to wait
I asked for love and

God gave me troubled people to help
I asked for favors and
God gave me opportunities
I received nothing I wanted

I received everything I needed
My Prayer Has Been Answered

~ Unknown

# The Tides of Providence

It's not what you gather, but what you sow,
That gives the heart a warming glow.
It's not what you get, but what you give,
Decides the kind of life you live.

It's not what you have,
But what you spare.
It's not what you take,
But what you share
That pays the greater dividend
And makes you richer in the end.

It's not what you spend upon yourself
Or hide away upon a shelf,
That brings a blessing for the day.
It's what you scatter by the way.

A wasted effort it may seem.
But what you cast upon the stream
Comes back to you recompense
Upon the tides of providence.

~ Patience Strong

# Don't Give It Up

Today life gave you another slap
but don't give it up
throwing your towel in the ring
for things gone wrong, for words that sting

'cos there must be another way
you will see it in the light of another day
When everything seems sour, not in your favour
look around until you find better flavour

so, don't just give but live it up
pick up the pieces, be tough
grind your teeth and turn another cheek
don't give it up, that's exactly what they seek

It's too easy to walk away
quitter never wins so you should better stay
look challenges straight in the eye
don't say yet the last good-bye

fight like an animal in a trap
but don't give it up

~ Z. Vujcic

# Handwriting On The Wall

A weary mother returned from the store,
Lugging groceries through the kitchen door.
Awaiting her arrival was her 8 year old son,
Anxious to relate what his younger brother had done.

While I was out playing and Dad was on a call,
T.J. took his crayons and wrote on the wall
It's on the new paper you just hung in the den.
I told him you'd be mad at having to do it again.

She let out a moan and furrowed her brow,
Where is your little brother right now?
She emptied her arms and with a purposeful stride,
She marched to his closet where he had gone to hide.

She called his full name as she entered his room.
He trembled with fear--he knew that meant doom
For the next ten minutes, she ranted and raved
About the expensive wallpaper and how she had saved.

Lamenting all the work it would take to repair,
She condemned his actions and total lack of care.
The more she scolded, the madder she got,
Then stomped from his room, totally distraught.

She headed for the den to confirm her fears.
When she saw the wall, her eyes flooded with tears.
The message she read pierced her soul with a dart.
It said, I love Mommy, surrounded by a heart.

Well, the wallpaper remained, just as she found it,
With an empty picture frame hung to surround it.
A reminder to her, and indeed to all,
Take time to read the handwriting on the wall.

~ Unknown

I slept and dreamt that life was joy
I awoke and found that life was duty
I acted, and behold!
Duty was joy.

~ Rabindranath Tagore

# The Most Beautiful Flower

The park bench was deserted as I sat down to read
Beneath the long, straggly branches of an old willow tree.
Disillusioned by life with good reason to frown,
For the world was intent on dragging me down.
And if that weren't enough to ruin my day,
A young boy out of breath approached me, all tired from play.
He stood right before me with his head tilted down
And said with great excitement, "Look what I found!"
In his hand was a flower, and what a pitiful sight,
With its petals all worn - not enough rain, or too little light.

Wanting him to take his dead flower and go off to play,
I faked a small smile and then shifted away.
But instead of retreating he sat next to my side
And placed the flower to his nose and declared with
overacted surprise,
"It sure smells pretty and it's beautiful, too.
That's why I picked it; here, it's for you."
The weed before me was dying or dead.
Not vibrant of colors: orange, yellow or red.
But I knew I must take it, or he might never leave.

So I reached for the flower, and replied, "Just what I need."
But instead of him placing the flower in my hand,
He held it mid-air without reason or plan.
It was then that I noticed for the very first time
That weed-toting boy could not see: he was blind.
I heard my voice quiver; tears shone in the sun

As I thanked him for picking the very best one.
"You're welcome," he smiled, and then ran off to play.

Unaware of the impact he'd had on my day.
I sat there and wondered how he managed to see
A self-pitying woman beneath an old willow tree.
How did he know of my self-indulged plight?
Perhaps from his heart, he'd been blessed with true sight.
Through the eyes of a blind child, at last I could see.

The problem was not with the world; the problem was me.
And for all of those times I myself had been blind,
I vowed to see the beauty in life,
And appreciate every second that's mine.
And then I held that wilted flower up to my nose
And breathed in the fragrance of a beautiful rose
And smiled as I watched that young boy,
Another weed in his hand,
About to change the life of an unsuspecting old man.

~ Unknown

# Our Deepest Fear

Our deepest fear is not that we are inadequate.
Our deepest fear is that we are powerful beyond measure.
It is our light, not our darkness
That most frightens us.

We ask ourselves
Who am I to be brilliant, gorgeous, talented, fabulous?
Actually, who are you not to be?
You are a child of God.

Your playing small
Does not serve the world.
There's nothing enlightened about shrinking
So that other people won't feel insecure around you.

We are all meant to shine,
As children do.
We were born to make manifest
The glory of God that is within us.

It's not just in some of us;
It's in everyone.

And as we let our own light shine,
We unconsciously give other people permission to do the
same.
As we're liberated from our own fear,
Our presence automatically liberates others.

~ Marianne Williamson

## *Love Comes With A Knife*

Love comes with a knife,
not some shy question,
and not with fears for its reputation!
I say these things disinterestedly.
Accept them in kind.

Love is a madman
working his wild schemes,
tearing off his clothes,
running through the mountains,
drinking poison,
and now quietly choosing annihilation.

A tiny spider tries to wrap an enormous wasp.
Think of the spiderweb woven across the cave
where Mohammad slept!
There are love stories,
and there is obliteration into love.

You've been walking the ocean's edge,
holding up your robes to keep them dry.

You must dive naked under and deeper under,
a thousand times deeper!
Love flows down.

The ground submits to the sky and suffers
what comes.
Tell me, is the earth worse
for giving in like that?

Don't put blankets over the drum!
Open completely.
Let your spirit-ear
listen to the green dome's passionate murmur.

Let the cords of your robe be untied.
Shiver in this new love beyond all
above and below.
The sun rises, but which way
does night go?
I have no more words.

Let soul speak with the silent
articulation of a face.

~ Rumi

*Watch*

Watch your thoughts, for they become words.
Watch your words, for they become actions.
Watch your actions, for they become habits.
Watch your habits, for they become character.
Watch your character, for it becomes your destiny.

~ Frank Outlaw

# That I A Better Person May Be

Light that lies deep inside of me
Come forth in all thy majesty
Show me thy gaze
Teach me thy ways
That I a better person may be

Darkness that lies deep inside of me
Come forth in all thy mystery
Show me thy gaze
Teach me thy ways
That I a better person may be

Love that lies deep inside of me
Come forth in all thy unity
Let me be thy gaze
Let me teach thy ways
That I a better person may be

~ Unknown

# May You Have Enough

May you have a healthy body,
To move around freely and roam wherever you desire to go.
May you have good vision,
To enjoy all the beauty the universe has to offer you.
May you have good listening ears,
To hear all the mighty tales and incredible stories that
make up life.
May you have a good sense of smell,
To inhale in all the rich aromas and fragrances floating in
the air.

May you have a warm sense of touch,
To give out loving hugs and comforting pats.
May you speak with kindness from your heart,
To soothe someone's hurt and to uplift someone's mood.
May you have lots of laughter,
To brighten up someone's day and make a difference.
May you have lots of courage,
To go after your dreams and turn them into reality.

May you have lots of love,
To spread around and leaving this world a better place.
May you have enough to feel blessed,
And to share your gift of blessings with others too.

~ Fion Lim

# The Misfits

Here's to the crazy ones.
The misfits.
The rebels.
The troublemakers.
The round pegs in the square holes.
The ones who see things differently.

They're not fond of rules.
And they have no respect for the status quo.
You can praise them, disagree with them, quote them,
disbelieve them, glorify or vilify them.

About the only thing you can't do is ignore them.
Because they change things.
They invent. They imagine. They heal.
They explore. They create. They inspire.
They push the human race forward.

And while some may see them as the crazy ones,
We see genius,
Because the ones who are crazy enough
To think that they can change the world,
Are the ones who do.

~ Steve Jobs

## Do More

Do more than belong: participate.
Do more than care: help.
Do more than believe: practice.
Do more than be fair: be kind.
Do more than forgive: forget.
Do more than dream: work.

~ William Arthur Ward

There's one sad truth in life I've found
While journeying east and west The
only folks we really wound
Are those we love the best.
We flatter those we scarcely know,
We please the fleeting guest,
And deal full many a thoughtless blow
To those who love us best.

~ Ella Wheeler Wilcox

For attractive lips,
Speak words of kindness.
For lovely eyes,
Seek out the good in people.
For a slim figure,
Share your food with the hungry.
For beautiful hair,
Let a child run his/her fingers through it once a day.
For poise,
Walk with the knowledge that you never walk alone.
People, even more than things,
Have to be restored, renewed, revived, reclaimed,
And redeemed; never throw out anyone.
Remember, if you ever need a helping hand,
You will find one at the end of each of your arms.
As you grow older, you will discover that you have two hands;
One for helping yourself, and the other for helping others.

~ Audrey Hepburn

# The Knots Prayer

Dear God:
Please untie the knots
that are in my mind,
my heart and my life.
Remove the have nots,
the can nots and the do nots
that I have in my mind.

Erase the will nots,
may nots,
might nots that may find
a home in my heart.

Release me from the could nots,
would nots and
should nots that obstruct my life.

And most of all,
Dear God,
I ask that you remove from my mind,
my heart and my life all of the 'am nots'
that I have allowed to hold me back,
especially the thought
that I am not good enough.
AMEN

~ Unknown

# A Heroes Creed "Did I"

Did I help someone to realize a dream
they thought they'd lost?
Did I listen when someone told me
the reward is worth the cost?
Did I praise someone for their efforts
and encourage someone toward their dreams?
Did I help someone to understand the end
never justifies the means?
Did I make someone laugh and smile
when they would much, rather frown?
Was I the one who picked them up
when everyone put them down?
Am I, the one they confide in
and know their conversations secure?
Did I provide them with someone to trust
in knowing their friendship will always endure?
Am I humble and constantly striving
to become more than I was yesterday?
Did I focus on the successes of others
and follow through with all that I say?
If I constantly strive to become
the one who can say I did to did I's.
Then my life is fulfilled,
knowing I have achieved life's greatest prize.

~ Carl Morris

## Little Things

Little stones make big mountains,
Little steps can cover miles,
Little acts of loving-kindness
Give the world it's biggest smiles.

Little words can soothe big troubles
Little hugs can dry big tears,
Little candles light the darkness,
Little memories last for years.

Little dreams can lead to greatness,
Little victories to success It's
the little things in life
That bring the greatest happiness.

~ Unknown

# A Stranger Passed By

I ran into a stranger as he passed by,
"Oh excuse me please" was my reply.
He said, "Please excuse me too;
I wasn't watching for you."

We were very polite, this stranger and I.
We went on our way and we said goodbye.
But at home a different story is told,
How we treat our loved ones, young and old.

Later that day, cooking the evening meal,
My son stood beside me very still.
When I turned, I nearly knocked him down.
"Move out of the way," I said with a frown.

He walked away, his little heart broken.
I didn't realize how harshly I'd spoken.
While I lay awake in bed,
God's still small voice came to me and said,

"While dealing with a stranger, common courtesy
you use,
but the family you love, you seem to abuse.
Go and look on the kitchen floor,
You'll find some flowers there by the door.
Those are the flowers he brought for you.
He picked them himself: pink, yellow and blue.

He stood very quietly not to spoil the surprise,
you never saw the tears that filled his little eyes."

By this time, I felt very small,
And now my tears began to fall.

I quietly went and knelt by his bed;
"Wake up, little one, wake up," I said.
"Are these the flowers you picked for me?"
He smiled, "I found 'em, out by the tree.

I picked 'em because they're pretty like you.
I knew you'd like 'em, especially the blue."
I said, "Son, I'm very sorry for the way I acted today;
I shouldn't have yelled at you that way."

He said, "Oh, Mom, that's okay.
I love you anyway."
I said, "Son, I love you too,
and I do like the flowers, especially the blue."

~ Unknown

# *If I Knew*

If I knew it would be the last time
I would be there to share your day,
well I'm sure you'll have so many more
so I can let just this one slip away.

For surely there's always tomorrow
to make up for an oversight,
and we always get a second chance
to make everything right.

There will always be another day
to say our," I love you"
And certainly there's another chance
to say our "Anything I can do?"

But just in case I might be wrong,
and today is all I get,
I'd like to say how much I love you
and I hope we never forget.

Tomorrow is not promised to anyone,
young or old alike,
And today may be the last chance
you get to hold your loved one tight.

So if you're waiting for tomorrow,
why not do it today?
For if tomorrow never comes,
you'll surely regret the day,

That you didn't take that extra time
for a smile, a hug, or a kiss
and you were too busy to grant someone,
what turned out to be their one last wish.

So always hold them dear.
Take time to say I'm sorry, Please forgive me,
Thank you, or It's okay.
And if tomorrow never comes,
you'll have no regrets about today.

~ Unknown

*The Serenity Prayer*

God grant that I might have
The courage to change the things I can,
The serenity to accept the things I cannot,
And the wisdom to know the difference

~ Reinhold Neibuhr

# *Beautiful Prayer*

I asked God to take away my habit.
God said, No.
It is not for me to take away, but for you to give it up.

I asked God to make my handicapped child whole.
God said, No.
His spirit is whole, his body is only temporary

I asked God to grant me patience.
God said, No.
Patience is a byproduct of tribulations;
it isn't granted, it is learned.

I asked God to give me happiness.
God said, No.
I give you blessings; Happiness is up to you.

I asked God to spare me pain.
God said, No.
Suffering draws you apart from worldly cares
and brings you closer to me.

I asked God to make my spirit grow.
God said, No.
You must grow on your own! ,
but I will prune you to make you fruitful.

I asked God for all things that I might enjoy life.
God said, No.
I will give you life, so that you may enjoy all things.

I ask God to help me LOVE others, as much as
He loves me.
God said...Ahhhh, finally you have the idea.

~ Joanne Gobure

Lord,
I crawled across the barrenness
To You
With my empty cup,
Uncertain in asking
Any small drop of refreshment.
If only I had known You better,
I'd have come running
With a bucket.

~ Nancy Spiegelberg

# I Choose The Mountain

The low lands call
I am tempted to answer
They are offering me a free dwelling
Without having to conquer

The massive mountain makes its move
Beckoning me to ascend
A much more difficult path
To get up the slippery bend

I cannot choose both
I have a choice to make
I must be wise
This will determine my fate

I choose, I choose the mountain
With all its stress and strain
Because only by climbing
Can I rise above the plane

I choose the mountain
And I will never stop climbing
I choose the mountain
And I shall forever be ascending

I choose the mountain

~ Howard Simon

I do not know
the day of the week
or the hour of the day.
I do not know
the measure of time
or the rate at which it flows
past me.
I cannot understand
the weight of a moment
or the duration of a year
All I know,
all I can comprehend
of the mathematics
of a life, are the times
your hand
is inside my hand,
and the times
it is not.

~ Tyler Knott Gregson

## Don't Dwell

Don't dwell on what might have been
or the chances you have missed.
Or the lonely nights that lie between
the last time lovers kissed.
Don't grasp too hard the memory
of the things that never came.
The door that did not open or
the wind that killed the flame.
There is still time enough to live...
And time enough to try again.
Be Happy.

~ Unknown

## In Myself

I do not ask for any crown
But that which all may win;
Nor try to conquer any world
Except the one within.
Be thou my guide until I find
Led by a tender hand,
The happy kingdom in myself
And dare to take command.

~ Louisa May Alcott

# Courage

When evening comes the shadows grow, as the sun begins
to set.
Take care that you don't come to know, a thing that's
called regret.
Not what you try or what you do, throughout a carefree
youth.
It's what you don't you'll come to rue, when time reveals
it's truth.

There is wisdom to be had from mistaken words and acts.
You'll find that failure's not so bad, it strengthens you in
fact.
Rejection's fear or the fear of failure, that paralizes you.
Is the stuff of tears and that which keeps you dreams
from coming true.

It takes a certain kind of nerve to tell someone you care.
But then nature tends to serve the person who would
dare.
Bravery isn't something you can cultivate from seed.
It must be conjured up anew each time that there's a
need.

So take these words and hold them close,
it's certain you'll find that,
one second of courage to speak from the heart
will result in you hearing them back.

~ Wish Belkin

# Forgiveness

If you try to reach inside of your heart
you can find forgiveness, or at least the start
And from that place where you can forgive
is where Hope, and Love, also thrive and live

And with each step that you try to take
and with that chance that your heart might break
Comes so much happiness, and so much strength
which Alone can carry you a fantastic length

For hate and anger will not get you there
and though you say that you just don't care
You can EASILY avoid the pain on which hate feeds
. . . the kind of hurt that No one needs

Just make the move, take that first stride
let go of the thing known as "Foolish Pride"
Maybe then you can start to repair the past
into something strong, that will mend, and last!

~ Barry S. Maltese

If I can stop one heart from breaking,
I shall not live in vain.
If I can ease one life the aching,
Or cool one pain,
Or help one fainting robin
Unto his nest again,
I shall not live in vain

~ Emily Dickinson

## The Challenge

Let others lead small lives,
But not you.
Let others argue over small things,
But not you.
Let others cry over small hurts,
But not you.
Let others leave their future
In someone else's hands,
But not you.

~ Jim Rohn

# Life's Tug Of War

Life can seem ungrateful and not always kind.
Life can pull at your heartstrings and play with your mind.
Life can be blissful and happy and free.
Life can put beauty in the things that you see.
Life can place challenges right at your feet.
Life can make good of the hardships we meet.
Life can overwhelm you and make your head spin.
Life can reward those determined to win.
Life can be hurtful and not always fair.
Life can surround you with people who care.
Life clearly does offer its ups and its downs.
Life's days can bring you both smiles and frowns.
Life teaches us to take the good with the bad.
Life is a mixture of happy and sad.

SO...
Take the life that you have and give it your best.
Think positive be happy let God do the rest.
Take the challenges that life has laid at your feet.
Take pride and be thankful for each one you meet.
To yourself give forgiveness if you stumble and fall.
Take each day that is dealt you and give it your all..
Take the love that you're given and return it with care.
Have faith that when needed it will always be there.
Take time to find the beauty in the things that you see.
Take life's simple pleasures let them set your heart free.
The idea here is simply to even the score.
As you are met and faced with Life's Tug of War.

~ Unknown

# *Attitude*

Success is a goal for all mankind,
Achieved through thought and a state of mind,
That strength of purpose we cannot exclude,
For success depends on our attitude.

So hear yourself, your voice within,
It will guide you through your life herein,
Six days of labour, one day of rest,
Shrug not your shoulders, do your best ...

Take not in life the mild approach,
The results you receive, you will not boast,
So give your all with plenty of drive,
For none of us leave this world alive.

Labour and learn in pursuit of your dreams,
The best things in life are all upstream,
What you put in, is what you get,
Pain of discipline beats regret.

Life is too long not to do well,
If you do not try, it's a living hell,
So play out your hand, enjoy the ride,
Don't live to regret, for not having tried.

~ C.N. Andre Day

# Footprints

One night I dreamed a dream.
I was walking along the beach with my Lord.
Across the dark sky flashed scenes from my life.
For each scene, I noticed two sets of footprints in the sand,
one belonging to me and one to my Lord.

When the last scene of my life shot before me
I looked back at the footprints in the sand.
There was only one set of footprints.
I realized that this was at the lowest and saddest
times of my life.
This always bothered me and I questioned the Lord
about my dilemma.

"Lord, You told me when I decided to follow You,
You would walk and talk with me all the way.
But I'm aware that during the most troublesome times
of my life there is only one set of footprints.
I just don't understand why, when I need You most,
You leave me."

He whispered, "My precious child,
I love you and will never leave you,
never, ever, during your trials and testings.
When you saw only one set of footprints,
It was then that I carried you.

~ Unknown

# You Are The Friend I Will Cherish

## Forever

Once in a long while,
someone special walks into your life
and really makes a difference.
They take the time
to show you in so many little ways
that you matter.
They see and hear the worst in you,
but don't walk away;
in fact, they may care more about you.
Their heart breaks with yours
their tears fall with yours
their laughter is shared with yours.

Once in a long while,
two special friends
have to go their separate ways.

Every time you see a certain gesture,
hear a certain laugh or phrase,
or return to a certain place,
it reminds you of them.
You treasure the time you had with them,
and you thank God that someone
can still touch your heart so deeply.

You remember their words, their looks,
their expressions;
you remember how much of themselves
they gave - not just to you, but to all.
You remember the strength
that amazed you.
the courage that impressed you.
the grace that inspired you,
and the love that touched you.

~ Laurie Winkelmann

It is in loving, not in being loved
The heart finds its quest
It is in giving, not in getting
Our lives are blest.

~ Unknown

# *Mothers Of The World*

Mothers of the world unite
And teach your children well,
Of the path that leads to Nirvana
Of the road that leads to hell.

Tell them of the pain that comes
From living an immoral life,
How drugs, nicotine and alcohol
Will lead to other strife.

That their body is a temple
Wherein the spirit dwells,
To treat it always with reverence and respect
Because God is there as well.

Teach them of the great ones
Who embody from age to age,
Who perfume the earth with their presence,
Leaving their mark on history's page.

Read with them the Bible,
The Bhagavad Gita when you can,
The Vedas, the Vishnu Puranas,
The Talmud and the Koran.

Tell them that humanity is one
Regardless of race, class or creed,
All pilgrims on the pathway to life
That leads to immortality.

Teach them to be kind to animals;
God trusts us with this tasks,
To give our love and pity
To those who cannot ask.

The birds of the air, the fish of the sea
All creatures that live, breathe and swim
Were created by the divine Lord
And all are loved by Him.

Example being the best teacher
Live up to the highest you can
Knowing the hand that rocks the cradle
Truly rules the world of man

~ Unknown

Christmas gift suggestions:
To your enemy, forgiveness.
To an opponent, tolerance.
To a friend, your heart.
To a customer, service.
To all, charity.
To every child, a good example.
To yourself, respect.

~ Oren Arnold

# I Am There - I Am Your Inner Light

Do you need me?
I am there
You cannot see me, yet I am the light you see by
You cannot hear me, yet I speak through your voice
You cannot feel me, yet I am the power at work in
your hands
I am at work, through you do not understand my ways
I am at work, though you do not recognize my works
I am not strange visions, I am no mysteries
Only in absolute stillness beyond self, can you know
Me as I am, and then but as feeling and a faith
Yet I am there. Yet I hear. Yet I answer.

When you need me, I am there
Even if you deny me, I am there
Even when you feel most alone, I am there
Even in your fears, I am there
I am there when you pray and when you do not
I am in you and you are in me
Only in your mind can you feel separate from me
For only in your mind are the mists of "yours" and
"mine"
Yet only with your mind can you know me and
experience me

Empty your hearts of empty fears:
When you get yourself out of the way, I am there
You can of yourself do nothing, but I can do all

And I am in all
Though you may not see the good, good is there
For I am there
I am there because I have to be, because I am

Only in me does the world have meaning
Only out of me dies the world take form
Only because of me does the world go forward
I am the law on which the movements of stars
And the growth of living cells are founded

I am the love that is the law's fulfilling
I am assurance. I am peace. I am oneness.
I am the law that you can live by
I am the love that you can cling to
I am your assurance, I am your peace
I am one with you, I am

Though you fail to find me, I do not fail you
Though your faith in me is unsure,
My faith in you never wavers
Because I know you, because I love you
Beloved I am there.

~ Willet Freeman

# Do It Anyway

People are often unreasonable, irrational, and self-centered.
Forgive them anyway.
If you are kind, people may accuse you of selfish,
ulterior motives.
Be kind anyway.
If you are successful,
you will win some unfaithful friends and some genuine
enemies.
Succeed anyway.
If you are honest and sincere people may deceive you.
Be honest and sincere anyway.
What you spend years creating,
others could destroy overnight.
Create anyway.
If you find serenity and happiness, some may be jealous.
Be happy anyway.
The good you do today, will often be forgotten.
Do good anyway.
Give the best you have, and it will never be enough.
Give your best anyway.
In the final analysis, it is between you and God.
It was never between you and them anyway.

~ Mother Teresa

# The Burning Dream

I dared to dream a burning dream,
of sounds unheard, of sights unseen;
a drum that tapped a different beat,
a growing flame, a burning.

I dared to stand when others bent.
I dared to go where no-one went.
I raised my head above the crowd,
I took a breath and cried aloud:

"I want to be a better me,
to be the best that I can be.
I want to walk beneath the sun
and do things I've left undone."

I took a step, and then one more.
I spread my wings, prepared to soar.
Some held me back. They thought me mad,
crazy, reckless; maybe bad.

But I kept my eyes upon my dream,
that sound unheard, that sight unseen,
and helping hands reached down for me
to lift me up, to set me free.

New friends saw what I could see;
said: "Be the best that you can be!
You can do it! We're proud of you!
So I spread my wings, and then... I FLEW.

~ Unknown

# On Children

Your children are not your children.
They are the sons and daughters of Life's longing
for itself.
They come through you but not from you,
And though they are with you yet they belong not
to you.

You may give them your love but not your
thoughts,
For they have their own thoughts.
You may house their bodies but not their souls,
For their souls dwell in the house of tomorrow,
which you cannot visit, not even in your dreams.
You may strive to be like them,
but seek not to make them like you.
For life goes not backward nor tarries with yesterday.

You are the bows from which your children
as living arrows are sent forth.
The archer sees the mark upon the path of the
infinite,
and He bends you with His might
that His arrows may go swift and far.
Let your bending in the archer's hand be for
gladness;
For even as He loves the arrow that flies,
so He loves also the bow that is stable.

~ Kahlil Gibran

# Hugs

It's wondrous what a hug can do.
A hug can cheer you when you're blue.
A hug can say, "I love you so," or
"Gee, I hate to see you go."

A hug is "Welcome back again," and
"Great to see you! Where've you been?"
A hug can soothe a small child's pain,
And bring a rainbow after rain.

The hug! There's just no doubt about it...
We scarcely could survive without it!
A hug delights and warms and charms
It must be why God gave us arms.

Hugs are great for fathers and mothers,
Sweet for sisters, swell for brothers.
And chances are your favorite aunts
Love them more than potted plants.

Kittens crave them; puppies love them;
Heads of state are not above them.
A hug can break the language barrier
And make your travels so much merrier.

No need to fret about your store of 'em;
The more you give, the more there's more of em!
So stretch those arms out without delay,
and give someone a hug today!

~ Unknown

# A Priceless Gift

Friendship is a priceless gift
that cannot be bought or sold,
But its value is far greater
than a mountain made of gold.

For gold is cold and lifeless,
it can neither see nor hear
And in the time of trouble
it is powerless to cheer.

It has no ears to listen
nor heart to understand,
It cannot bring you comfort
or reach out a helping hand.

So when you ask God for a gift
Be thankful if He sends
Not diamonds, pearls, or riches
But the love of real true friends.

~ Helen Steiner Rice

# The Guest House

This being human is a guesthouse
Every morning a new arrival
A joy, a depression, a meanness
Some momentary awareness
Comes as an unexpected visitor

Welcome and entertain them all!
Even if they're a crowd of sorrows
Who violently sweep your house
Empty of its furniture
Still treat each guest honorably
He may be cleaning you out
For some new delight!

The dark thought, the shame, the malice
Meet them at the door laughing
And invite them in
Be grateful for whoever comes
Because each has been sent
As a guide from the beyond

~ Rumi

## Conversation

God and I in space alone
and nobody else in view.
"And where are the people, O Lord," I said,
"the earth below and the sky o'er head
and the dead whom once I knew?"

"That was a dream," God smiled and said,
"A dream that seemed to be true.
There were no people, living or dead,
there was no earth, and no sky o'er head;
there was only Myself – in you."

"Why do I feel no fear," I asked,
"meeting You here this way?
For I have sinned I know full well-and
is there heaven, and is there hell,
and is this the Judgment Day?"

"Nay, those were but dreams,"
the Great God said,
"Dreams that have ceased to be.
There are no such things as fear or sin;
there is no you – you never have been-there
is nothing at all
but Me."

~ Ella Wheeler Wilcox

# Leadership

The leader is best,
When people are hardly aware of his existence,
Not so good when people praise his government,
Less good when people stand in fear,
Worst, when people are contemptuous.
Fail to honor people, and they will fail to honor you.
But of a good leader,
who speaks little When his work is done,
his aim fulfilled,
The people say, 'We did it ourselves.'

~ LaoTzu

Kind hearts are the gardens,
Kind thoughts are the roots,
Kind words are the flowers,
Kind deeds are the fruits.

Take care of your garden
And keep out the weeds,
Fill it with sunshine
Kind words and kind deeds.

~ Henry Wadsworth Longfellow

# Our True Heritage

The cosmos is filled with precious gems.
I want to offer a handful of them to you this
morning.
Each moment you are alive is a gem,
shining through and containing earth and sky,
water and clouds.

It needs you to breathe gently
for the miracles to be displayed.
Suddenly you hear the birds singing,
the pines chanting,
see the flowers blooming,
the blue sky,
the white clouds,
the smile and the marvelous look
of your beloved.

You, the richest person on Earth,
who have been going around begging for a living,
stop being the destitute child.
Come back and claim your heritage.
We should enjoy our happiness
and offer it to everyone.
Cherish this very moment.
Let go of the stream of distress
and embrace life fully in your arms.

~ Thich Nhat Hanh

# Better To Light Candles

It is better to light candles
than to curse the darkness.
It is better to plant seeds
than to accuse the earth.
The world needs all of our power
and love and energy,
and each of us has something that we can give.
The trick is to find it and use it,
to find it and give it away.
So there will always be more.
We can be lights for each other,
and through each other's illumination
we will see the way.
Each of us is a seed,
a silent promise,
and it is always spring.

~ Merle Shain

# Who Are My People

My people? Who are they?
I went into the church where the congregation
Worshiped my God. Were they my people?
I felt no kinship to them as they knelt there.

My people! Where are they?
I went into the land where I was born,
Where men spoke my language...
I was a stranger there.
'My people,' my soul cried. 'Who are my people?'

Last night in the rain I met an old man
Who spoke a language I do not speak,
Which marked him as one who does not know my
God.
With apologetic smile he offered me
The shelter of his patched umbrella.
I met his eyes... And then I knew.

~ Rosa Zagnoni Marinoni

# Judge Gently

Pray don't find fault with the man who limps
or stumbles along the road,
unless you have worn the shoes he wears
or struggled beneath his load.
There may be tacks in his shoes that hurt,
though hidden away from view,
or the burden he bears, placed on your back
might cause you to stumble too.
Don't sneer at the man who's down today
unless you have felt the blow
that caused his fall or felt the shame
that only the fallen know.
You may be strong, but still the blows
that were his if dealt to you,
in the selfsame way, at the selfsame time,
might cause you to stagger too.
Don't be too harsh with the man who sins
or pelt him with word or stone,
unless you are sure, yea, doubly sure,
that you have no sins of your own for
you know perhaps if the tempter's voice
should whisper as softly to you
as it did to him when he went astray,
it might cause you to stumble too.

~ Unknown

# *Raising Our Children*

If we tell our children they're so bad,
They'll grow up as we hope they never had.
But if we tell our children they're so good,
They'll grow up exactly as we hope they would.

If our expectations of them are low,
In their performance it'll show.
But if our expectations of them are high,
They'll stretch and reach for the sky.

If we don't openly show them affection,
It could lead to a misconception.
But if we show them love through touch,
They'll grow close to us.

If with them we hardly talk,
Then at what we say they'll baulk.
But if with them we'll join and play,
Then, as a family, together we'll stay.

~ Virend Singh

# A Special Favour

Now that you have finished reading this book, please consider writing a review. To an author, reviews are GOLD. They help readers discover interesting new books. I would truly appreciate your appraisal. Please go to the book page on Amazon.com, scroll to the bottom of the Customer Reviews section and "Write a customer review".

---

# You're Invited

If you want more of the kind of information contained in this book, join our community and receive regular doses of "The Hidden Truths", our monthly newsletter. As a reward for becoming a member you will receive a free copy of *The Ultimate Success Formula: Finally, a Formula That Reveals the Secret Behind EVERY Great Success!* as well as another surprise gift. Membership is free!

Go now to www.TheInexplicableLawsOfSuccess.com/optin/ and claim your free gifts.

---

# Acknowledgements

We'd like to thank those who have shared with us many of the poems and verses used in this book. These have been gathered over the past 20+ years from emails, newsletters, ezines, blog posts, web pages, audio clips, etc. Hence, like any book of quotations, some sources are obscure and citations are not available.

# Other resources by Verusha Singh

*The Inexplicable Laws Of Success – Discover the Hidden Truths that Separate the 'Best' from the 'Rest'* **(Classic Edition)** available from Amazon in hardcover, softcover and e-book formats. Offering powerful insights into the reality that separate the 'Best' from the 'Rest', *The Inexplicable Laws of Success* is perhaps the first and only self-help book that provides a complete map or picture of what it takes to be truly successful in life. Using proprietary (trademarked) concepts, it explains the process of success and achievement in an unconventional yet exciting way.

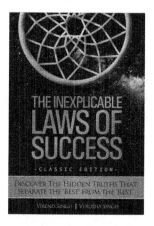

PROFESSIONAL ENDORSEMENTS:

"I am continually amazed by Verusha's passion to assist individuals in their personal growth. She writes in way that is motivating and inspirational."

**- Deepak Chopra, International Best-Selling Author**

"This book gives ideas and insights into unlocking and releasing your full potential for happiness and success."

**- Brian Tracy, International Best-Selling Author**

The **Workbook** is a great self-study course to accompany the Classic Edition. It is a practical tool that guides the reader/student through the content. The exercises are planned to help reinforce the key learning points in each chapter. For a trainer, it is a very useful reference manual and guide.

The **Pocket Edition** (of *The Inexplicable Laws of Success*) is an abridged version for readers who want the content in fewer words while retaining the essence of the original. A digital version of the Pocket Edition is not available for sale. A softcover version may be purchased from Amazon by clicking the image below.

*Inspirational Words and Positive Quotes to Live By: An Insightful Collection of Motivational Quotes* is packed with wisdom and serve to remind you that life can be good, no matter what challenges you may be facing. These quotes will empower and encourage you to live your life to the fullest. They come from accomplished people, sages, philosophers and thinkers, all of whom started out as an ordinary citizens and have achieved greatness.

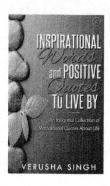

*Inspirational Short Stories about Success and Happiness: Insightful Words of Wisdom to Uplift the Heart and Reawaken the Spirit.* Everyone, at some point in their lives, feels overwhelmed by the challenges and obstacles that they have to face. In times of difficulty, we often look around to find a source of inspiration and hope. Sometimes the easiest and most powerful way to get a message across is through a story. Stories hold our attention and stay with us long after we have heard them. *Inspirational Short Stories about Success and Happiness* will inspire and uplift readers with its stories of optimism, faith, and strength.

# About The Author

**Verusha** Singh is a writer and entrepreneur who operates her own self-publishing business. She has qualifications in Media and Writing, and Editing and Publishing. After graduating from university she held positions at two publishing companies, including Hay House (Australia). Verusha's plans for the future are to continue to write and teach about all aspects of success.

---

# Let's Connect

- Visit www.TheInexplicableLawsOfSuccess.com
- Download free chapters of our flagship publication: *The Inexplicable Laws of Success: Discover the Hidden Truths that Separate the 'Best' from the 'Rest' (Classic Edition).*
- Connect with us on Facebook, Twitter, YouTube and LinkedIn via the website
- Subscribe to our newsletter – 'The Hidden Truths'
- Read our blog posts

---

**For more resources by Verusha go to**
www.inkNivory.com/resources/

CPSIA information can be obtained
at www.ICGtesting.com
Printed in the USA
BVOW10s1053301117
501625BV00022B/1053/P